Written by Marie Farré
Illustrated by Henri Galeron

*Specialist adviser:
Dr Jane Mainwaring,
The British Museum
(Natural History)*

*ISBN 1 85103 060 3
First published 1989 in the United Kingdom by
Moonlight Publishing Ltd,
131 Kensington Church Street, London W8*

© *1988 by Editions Gallimard
Translated by Sarah Matthews
English text* © *1989 by Moonlight Publishing Ltd
Typeset by Saxon Printing Ltd, Derby
Printed in Italy by La Editoriale Libraria*

POCKET • WORLDS

Prehistoric Animals

What animals walked the Earth millions of years ago, long before there were people?

THE ANIMAL WORLD

About 200 million years ago, dinosaurs ruled the Earth.

There were no people then, only different kinds of reptiles. The name 'dinosaur' means 'terrible lizard'. Some of them were the biggest animals that have ever lived, taller than lamp-posts, taller than houses. Have you ever seen dinosaurs in cartoons or science-fiction films? They are often shown as huge and terrifying – but they are not often shown as they really were. For instance, **Tyrannosaurus rex**, on the opposite page, is drawn about three times the size it was in real life. But even though it was a great deal smaller, it was certainly very fierce.

Not all dinosaurs were frightening, though, and not all of them were big.

How do we know what they were like? To find out what people were like in past times, we can explore their buildings, look at what they made and read what they wrote. That is history. But in prehistoric times nobody wrote things down. To find out how things were then, we have to look carefully at fossils.

This scientist has gone down into a cave to look at fossils of prehistoric plants and animals.

These researchers have found some dinosaur bones. Some of them are much bigger than the people who have found them!

These fossils date from about 500 million years ago.

What is a fossil?

Fossils are the remains of plants and animals which were buried in the mud or sand of seas and lakes millions of years ago. Bit by bit, the soft parts of the plant or animal rotted away. Only the hard parts, the veins of a leaf, or the bones or shells of animals were left.

These are fossils of animals which lived about 280 million years ago.

As thousands of years passed, more and more mud and sand pressed down on the remains. The hard parts of the bodies were replaced by stone. Usually, the deeper down a fossil is found, the older it is. The first fossils are 600 million years old.

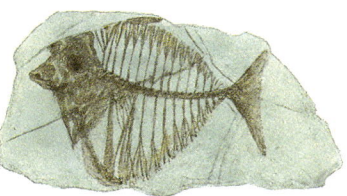

About 200 million years ago, these fossils of a fish and a frog were formed.

How life began on Earth: we think that, 4,000 million years ago, water began to collect on the surface of the cooling Earth; the sea was formed.

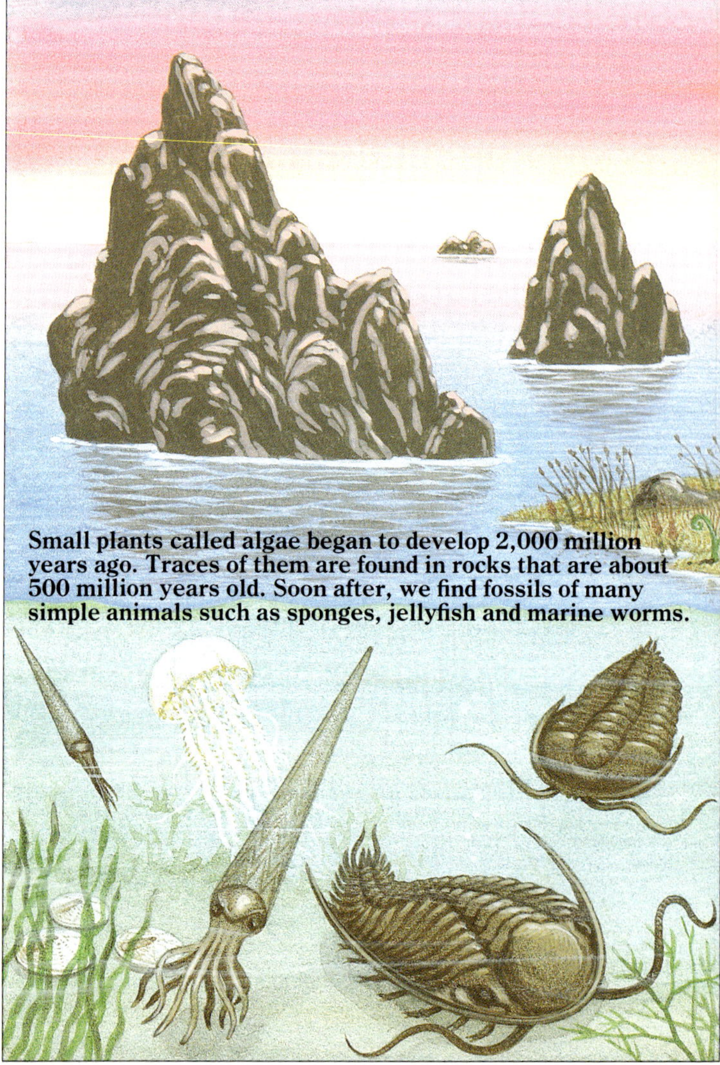

Small plants called algae began to develop 2,000 million years ago. Traces of them are found in rocks that are about 500 million years old. Soon after, we find fossils of many simple animals such as sponges, jellyfish and marine worms.

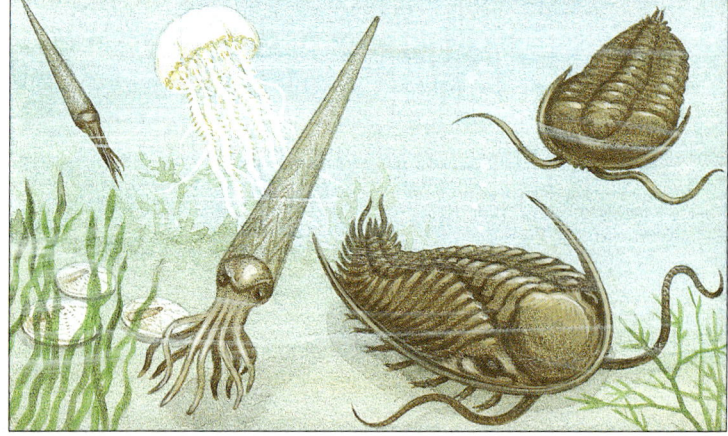

The first plants that grew on land and had proper roots were ferns. Some of them were as tall as trees. Before they developed there were only mosses, growing along the edges of streams and lakes.

Snails and other shelled animals developed in the sea. **Trilobites**, animals a bit like woodlice, grubbed around in the mud, while simple fish swam through the warm water.

About 285 million years ago, some creatures lifted their heads out of the water and learnt to breathe air. Crawling out on to land, these animals could live in damp places, but they returned to the water to breed. Today we call animals like this **amphibians.**

13

Hylonomus, one of the earliest of all reptiles, looked a little like a lizard.

The arrival of reptiles

Reptiles are animals that creep or crawl along the ground. Their bodies are covered by a waterproof, scaly skin. Reptiles have to bask in the sun to collect the heat that gives them the energy to move around. This means that they have to live in hot climates. Hundreds of millions of years ago there were many, many more types of reptile than there are today. The dinosaurs are the most famous, but there were many other kinds living at the same time too. Today, four main groups of reptile still survive on the Earth: tortoises, lizards, snakes and crocodiles.

Cynognathus, with its long curved teeth, was a mammal-like reptile that lived just before the dinosaurs.

Dimetrodons had long spines on their backs, covered with skin to make a kind of sail. As the sun rose in the morning, it warmed the blood in *Dimetrodon*'s skin sail. Then *Dimetrodon* was able to wake up and start to hunt while its reptile prey were all still sleepy with the cold.

In the sea and under it

Ichthyosaurs are one group of ancient reptiles that spent all their time in the sea. They looked a bit like our modern dolphins. Their bodies were streamlined so that they could swim very fast, but they had to come up to the surface to breathe air. Unlike other reptiles, which laid eggs on land, the ichthyosaurs gave birth to live babies in the water. Baby ichthyosaurs were born tail-first, just as dolphins are today.

A hungry Mosasaur finds itself outnumbered by Plesiosaurs.

Plesiosaurs had very long necks and small heads; their jaws were full of sharp, pointed teeth. They probably caught fish.

Some people think the Lock Ness Monster could be a plesiosaur!

Huge *Pteranodon* soared over the ocean. The crest on its head stopped it tipping into the sea as it dived down for fish, which it ate or tucked into the pouch under its beak for storage, just as a pelican does today. It had a wingspan of about 7 metres, and it weighed as much as 30 kilos.

What's scaly, with sharp teeth, and can fly?

Pterosaurs were probably warm-blooded, more like bats than reptiles and may have had furry bodies.

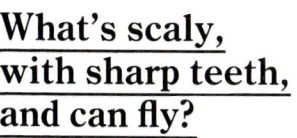

Pterosaurs lived at the same time as dinosaurs. Dinosaurs dominated the land, and pterosaurs ruled in the air. They had no feathers to help them fly, as modern birds do, but glided on large broad wings of scaly skin. They probably lived in trees, using air-currents to swoop down on their prey.

The ancestor of our modern birds was probably *Archaeopteryx*. From a fossil found in Germany, scientists have deduced that it probably looked like this, with feathers like a bird and teeth like a reptile.

The age of the dinosaurs

Dinosaurs first developed about 225 million years ago, and dominated the Earth until they died out about 64 million years ago. Dinosaurs were land-living reptiles. The great thing about them was that they were able to walk and run very well, because of the way their legs were tucked in underneath their bodies. There were a great many different kinds of dinosaur, from huge, slow-moving plant-eaters to the quicker, razor-toothed meat-eaters.

A baby dinosaur hatches out. A lot of fossilised dinosaur eggs have been preserved.

Like reptiles today, dinosaurs laid eggs and had to keep them warm until they were ready to hatch. Some dinosaur parents stayed with their eggs, and fetched food for their young when they hatched.

Dinosaurs through the ages
These are some of the dinosaurs that developed during the 160 million years they walked the Earth.

1. *Anchisaurus* 2. *Mamenchisaurus*
3. *Stegosaurus* 4. *Allosaurus*
5. *Deinonychus* 6. Ankylosaurid
7. *Spinosaurus* 8. *Edmontosaurus*
9. *Chasmosaurus*

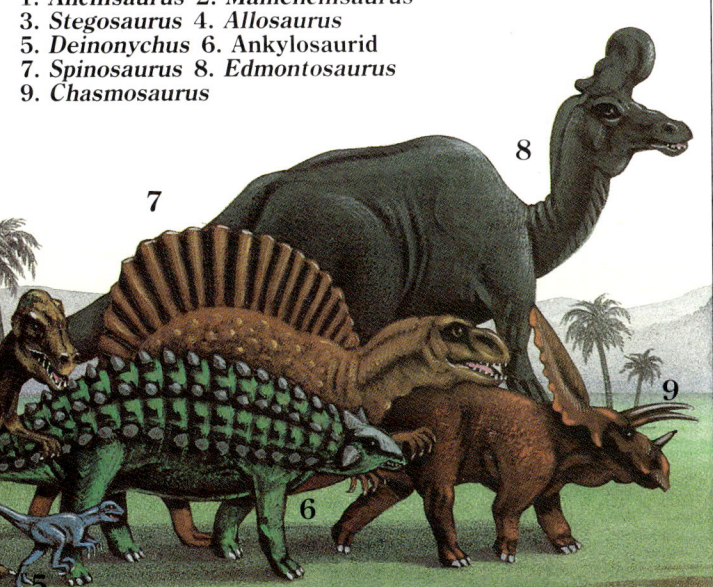

The world during the age of the dinosaur was a much warmer, lusher place. There was never a shortage of plant food for huge plant-eaters like *Apatosaurus* to feed on.

In this picture you can see lumbering **Apatosaurus**, which weighed as much as six elephants, sharp-clawed **Allosaurus**, a **tortoise**, tiny **Ornitholestes**, and **Stegosaurus** with its armoured back.

As well as having an armoured back, *Stegosaurus* had four sharp horns at the end of its tail.

Ankylosaurus had a massive club at the end of its tail, which it could thump down on attackers.

As the carnivores developed, they grew longer and stronger claws, and more and more pointed, razor-sharp teeth. The placid plant-eaters needed ever more exotic armour to protect them, until they were plodding around like vegetarian tanks. Some carnivores, like these **Tyrannosaurus rex**, developed enormously strong back legs, so that they could stand upright and run. Their front legs were tiny and useless, as they didn't reach their mouths.

Triceratops had an enormously heavy head, with a bony frill and three sharp horns.

Why did dinosaurs die out?

It is one of the great mysteries of the world. Dinosaurs appeared about 225 million years ago, developed in all sorts of different, highly successful ways for 160 million years, and then died out, until there were none left alive at all.

People have come up with all sorts of different theories to explain why dinosaurs became extinct. Some think that the Earth's surface shifted, and the climate and conditions of life changed so completely that the dinosaurs no longer fitted in to the world as it had become.

The skeleton of *Megatherium*. This mammal-like animal survived while the dinosaurs died out.

Another possibility is that cosmic rays bombarded the Earth from space, and killed whole ranges of animals which were alive then. A third theory suggests that over thousands and thousands of years the world gradually became much cooler. In the cold, the reptilian dinosaurs could not keep warm, or move fast enough to catch their prey. **None of the theories quite answers all the questions.** In time, perhaps, scientists will find an answer to this extraordinary puzzle.

Uintatherium was an early mammal which looked something like our modern rhinoceros. It had three pairs of horns, and long, horny toe-nails.

As the climate changed, the dense, moist forests died out, and vast grasslands developed. Over the plains ran huge, flightless birds like this **Phororhacos**. It looked a little like the ostriches we know today, except that it had enormous sharp claws on its feet, and a sharp beak for slashing and biting at the snakes and small mammals it liked to eat. Particularly tasty was **Megazostrodon**, a kind of tiny early mammal which looked like the modern shrew.

The dinosaurs were dying out, and **mammals** were stepping into the gap they left. Mammals are animals which give birth to live babies, rather than eggs, and which suckle their babies with milk. Their bodies are covered with hair. Mammals tended to have bigger brains than dinosaurs. These early mammals were the ancestors of almost all the animals we know on Earth today, including human beings.

About two million years ago, a great Ice Age gripped the Earth.

The climate cooled down, and the glaciers stretched out from both the Poles until huge areas of land and sea were covered in ice and snow. Only the hardiest of animals could live in these conditions.

Among those that did survive and thrive was **the mammoth**, which stood over four metres high, and had tusks more than five metres long. It lived on the plains of North America. One of the few animals which attacked the mammoth was **Smilodon**, the sabre-toothed tiger. It used its huge canines to slash at its prey and kill it. But the greatest hunter of them all had now appeared on the scene. Early people had developed, and had learnt to use tools and traps to catch animals much bigger and more powerful than they were. The age of the giants was over; the age of cleverness had begun.

Gluptodon was an enormous plant-eater which lived in South America.

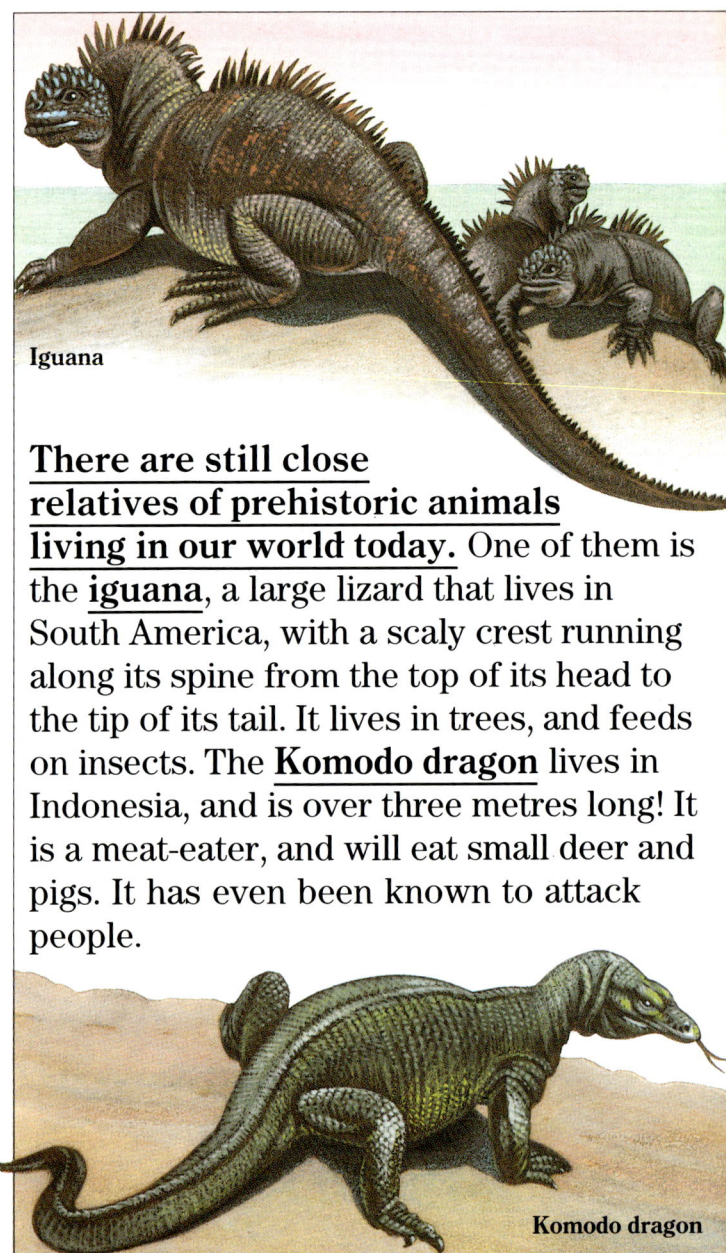

Iguana

<u>**There are still close relatives of prehistoric animals living in our world today.**</u> One of them is the **<u>iguana</u>**, a large lizard that lives in South America, with a scaly crest running along its spine from the top of its head to the tip of its tail. It lives in trees, and feeds on insects. The **<u>Komodo dragon</u>** lives in Indonesia, and is over three metres long! It is a meat-eater, and will eat small deer and pigs. It has even been known to attack people.

Komodo dragon

Duck-billed platypus

The **duck-billed platypus** lives in Australia. It is a mixture of reptile and mammal – it lays eggs, but then it suckles its babies with milk when they hatch out. The **pangolin** is a kind of ant-eater which lives in South America, and has a scaly back and a hairy belly. It uses its long sticky tongue to catch the ants and termites which it feeds on. **Crocodiles** have survived from prehistoric times too. Neither changing climate nor changing habitat could threaten them, until people came along to kill them for their skins...

Pangolin

Would you like to play the Evolution Game? Take a dice and some counters. Start at the beginning of the world, and play with your friends to see who can arrive first at the age of the human hunter!

Index

Allosaurus, 21, 23
Anchisaurus, 21
ankylosaurid, 21
Ankylosaurus, 25
Apatosaurus, 22, 23
Archaeopteryx, 19
Chasmosaurus, 21
crocodiles, 14, 33
Cynognathus, 14
Dimetrodons, 15
dinosaurs, 7, 20-25; dying out, 26-27, 29
Deinonychus, 21
Edmontosaurus, 21
fossils, 7-9
Gluptodon, 30
ichthyosaurs, 16
Mamenchisaurus, 21

mammals, 29
mammoths, 30
Megatherium, 27
Megozostrodon, 29
mosasaurs, 16
ornitholestes, 23
Phororhacos, 29
plesiosaurs, 16-17
pteranodons, 18
pterosaurs, 19
reptiles, 14, 21
Smilodons, 30
spinosaurus, 21
Stegosaurus, 21, 23, 25
tortoises, 14, 23
Triceratops, 25
Tyrannosaurus rex, 7, 25
Uintatherium, 27

Now read more '**Animal World**' titles
in the **Pocket Worlds** series:

All About Pigs
Crocodiles and Alligators
Animals in Winter
Bees, Ants and Termites
Wild Life in Towns
Teeth and Fangs
The Long Life and Gentle Ways of the Elephant
Animals Underground
Big Bears and Little Bears
Big Cats and Little Cats
Wolf!
Cows and Their Cousins
Monkeys and Apes
Animal Colours and Patterns